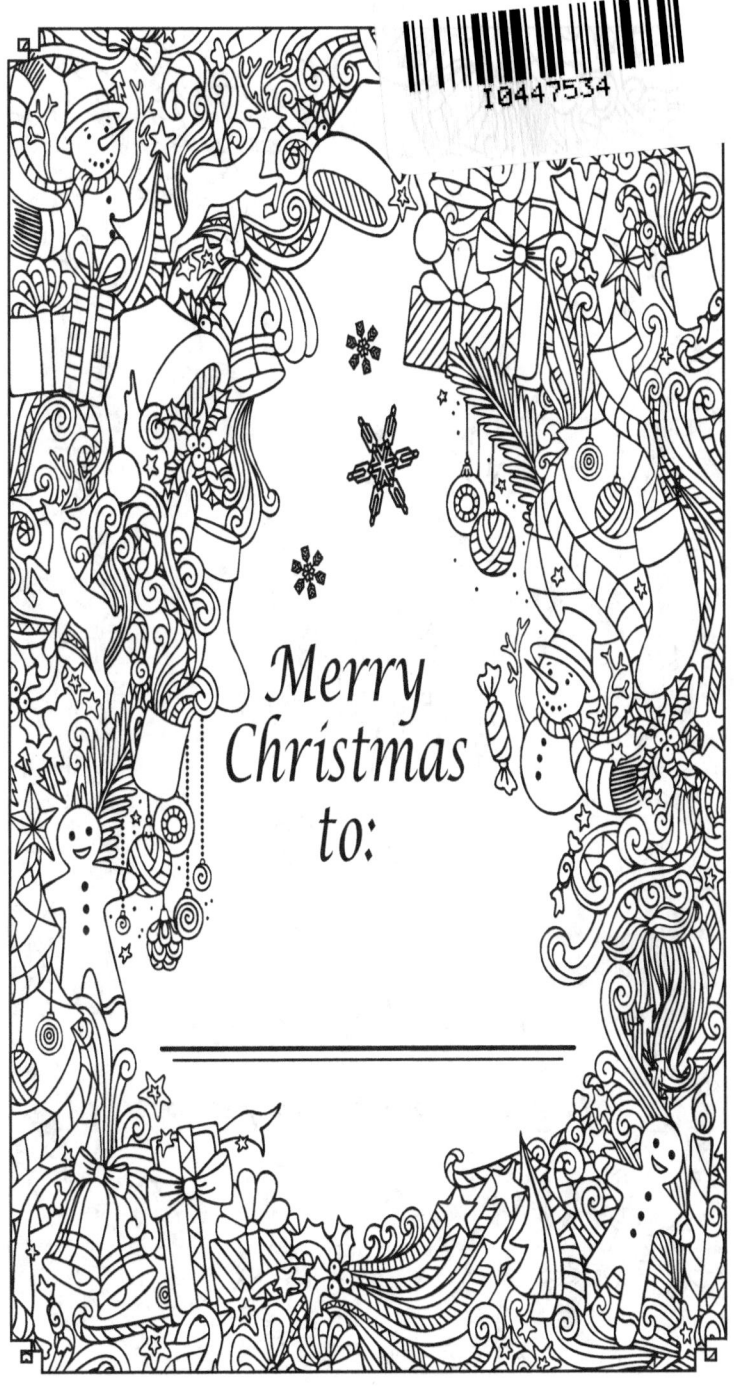

Merry
Christmas
to:

_____

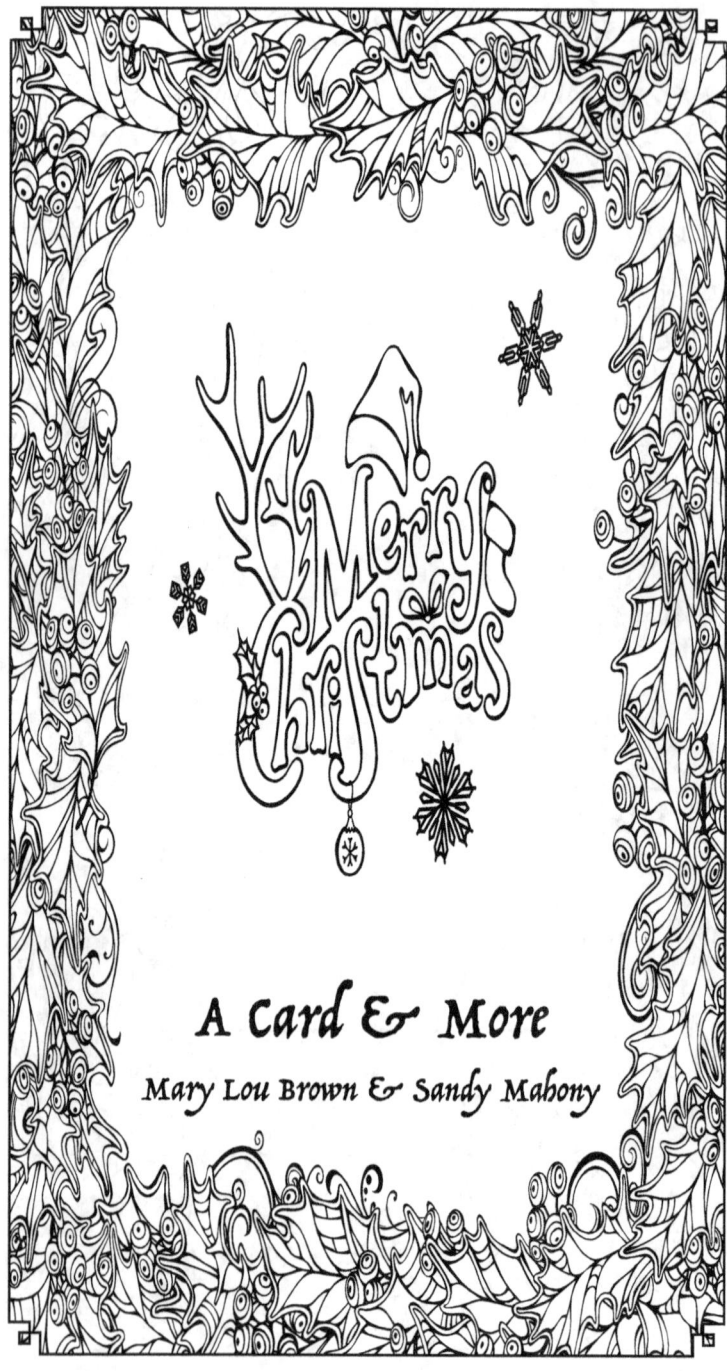

Merry Christmas

A Card & More

Mary Lou Brown & Sandy Mahony

Celebrate the Season!

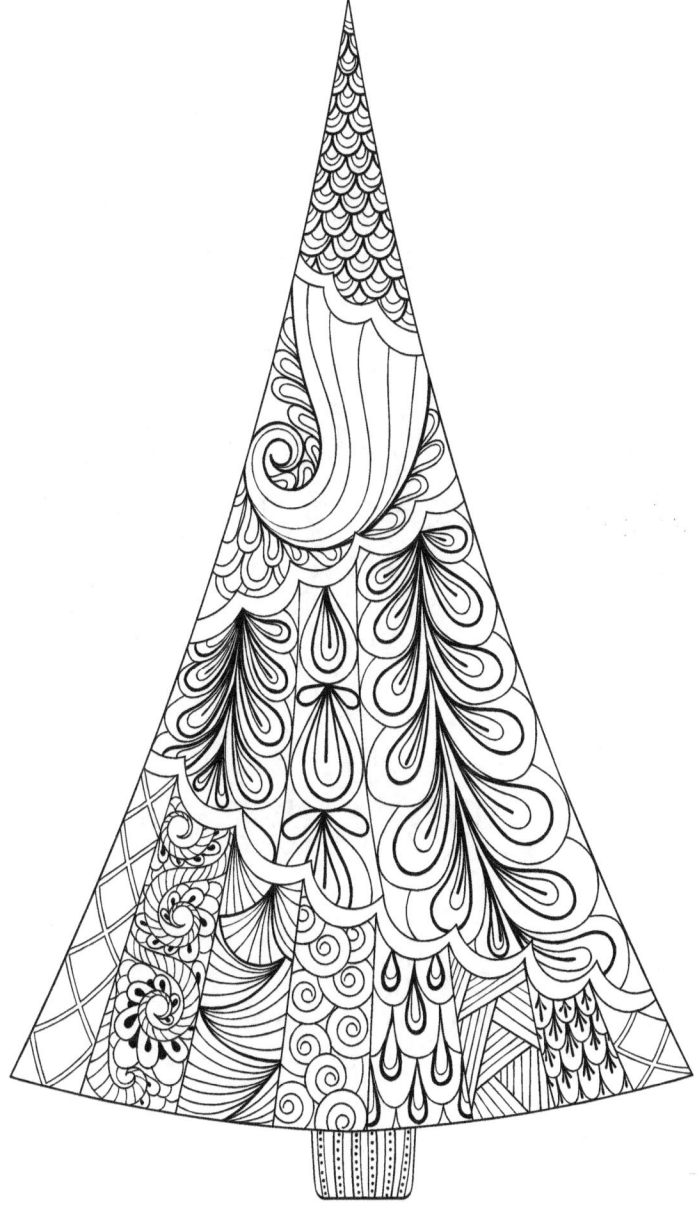

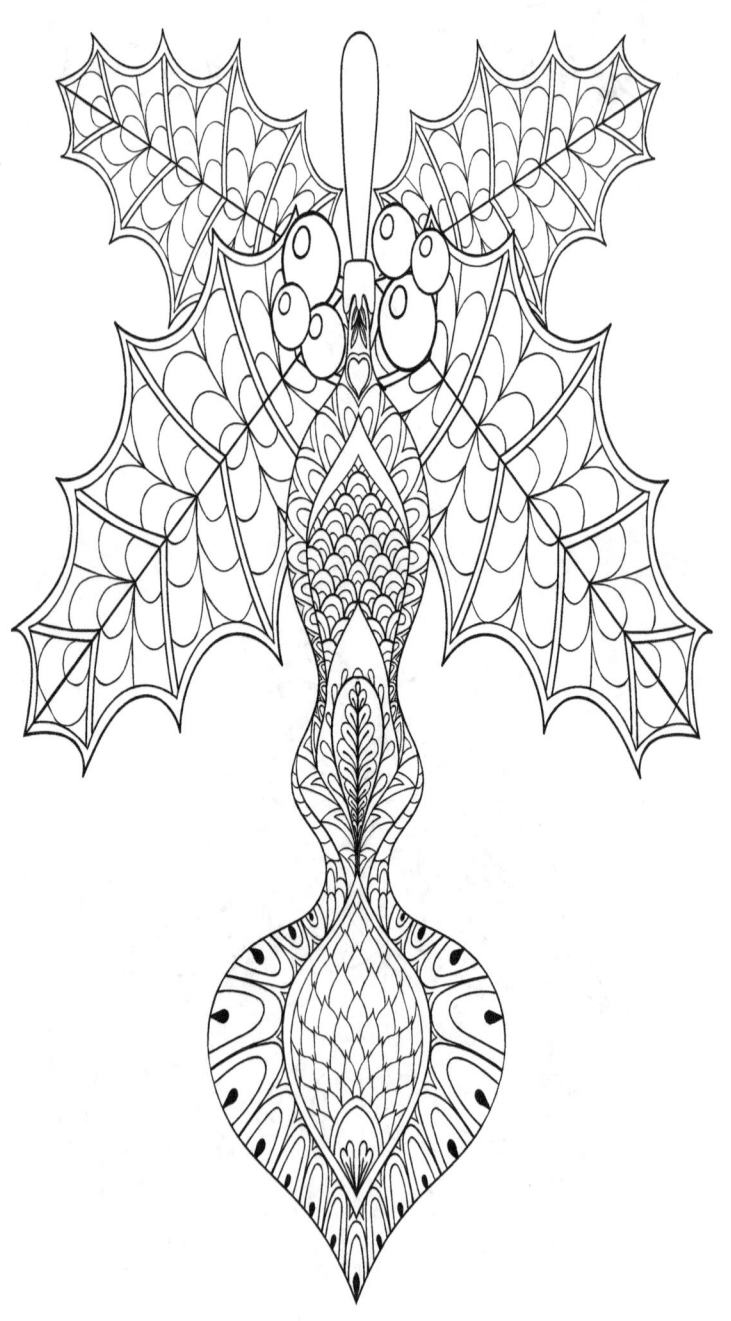

Oh, Oh, the Mistletoe!

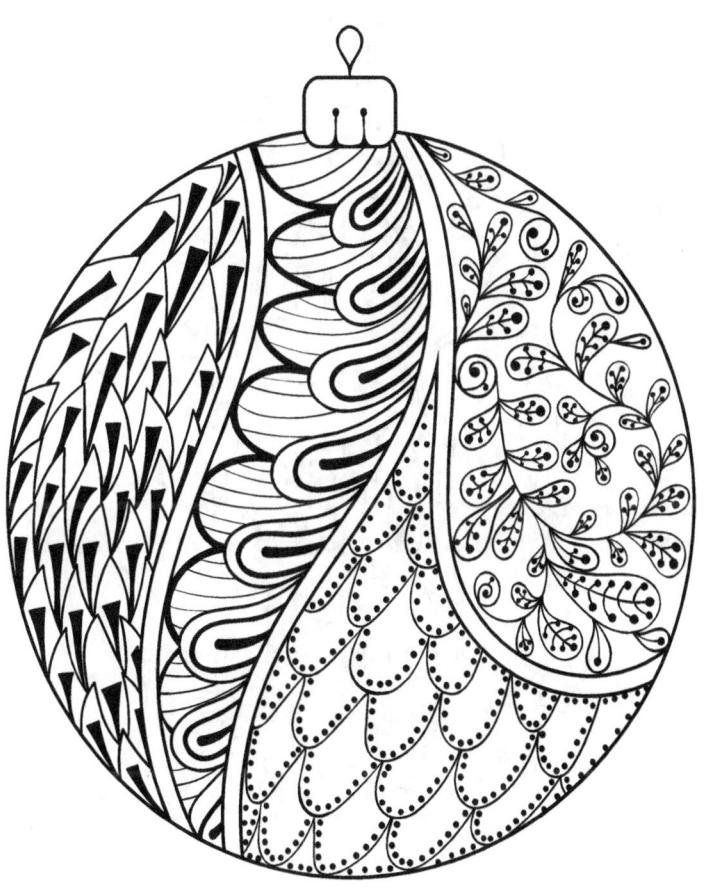

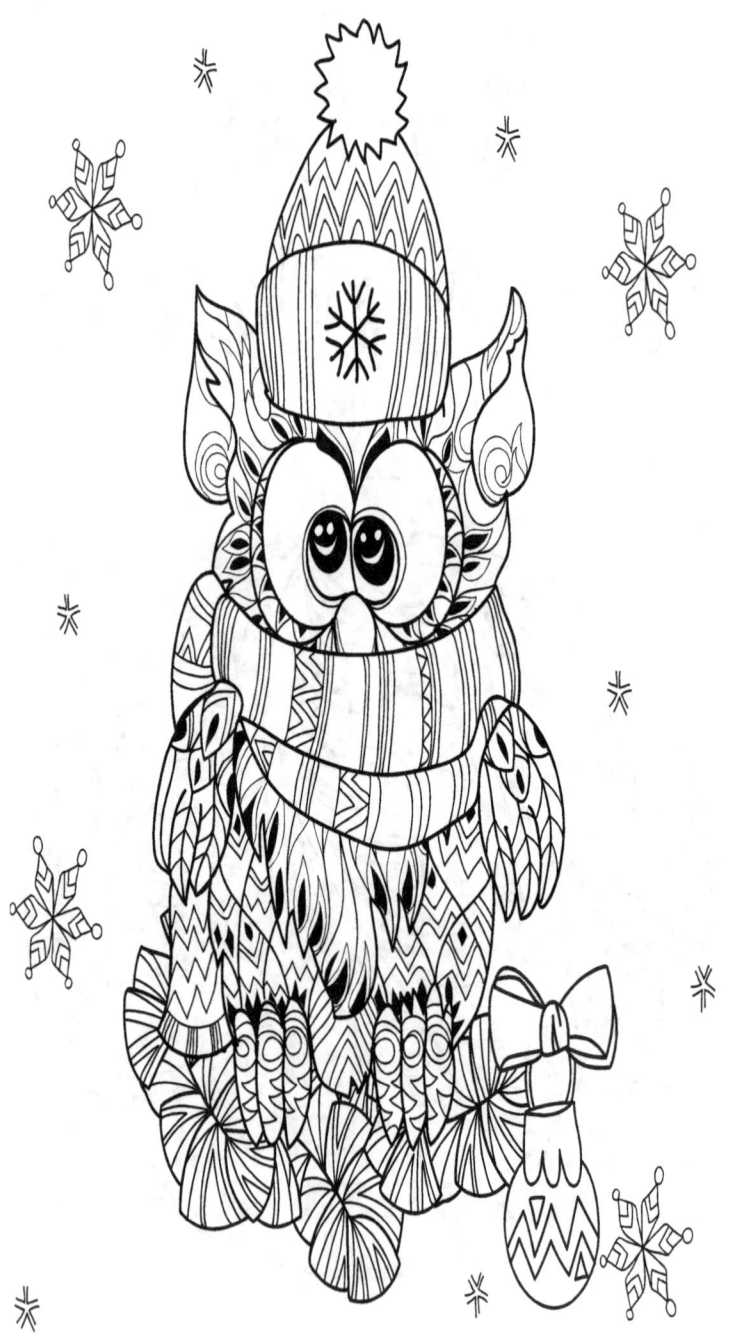

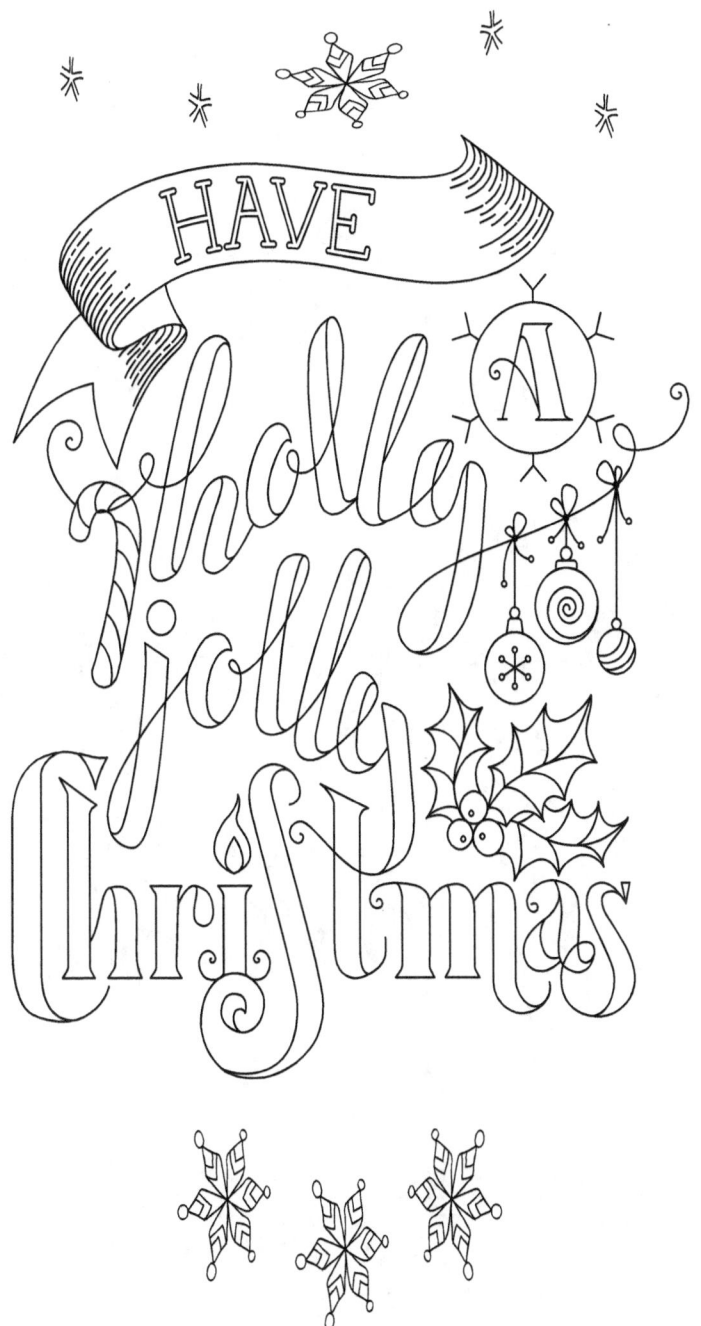

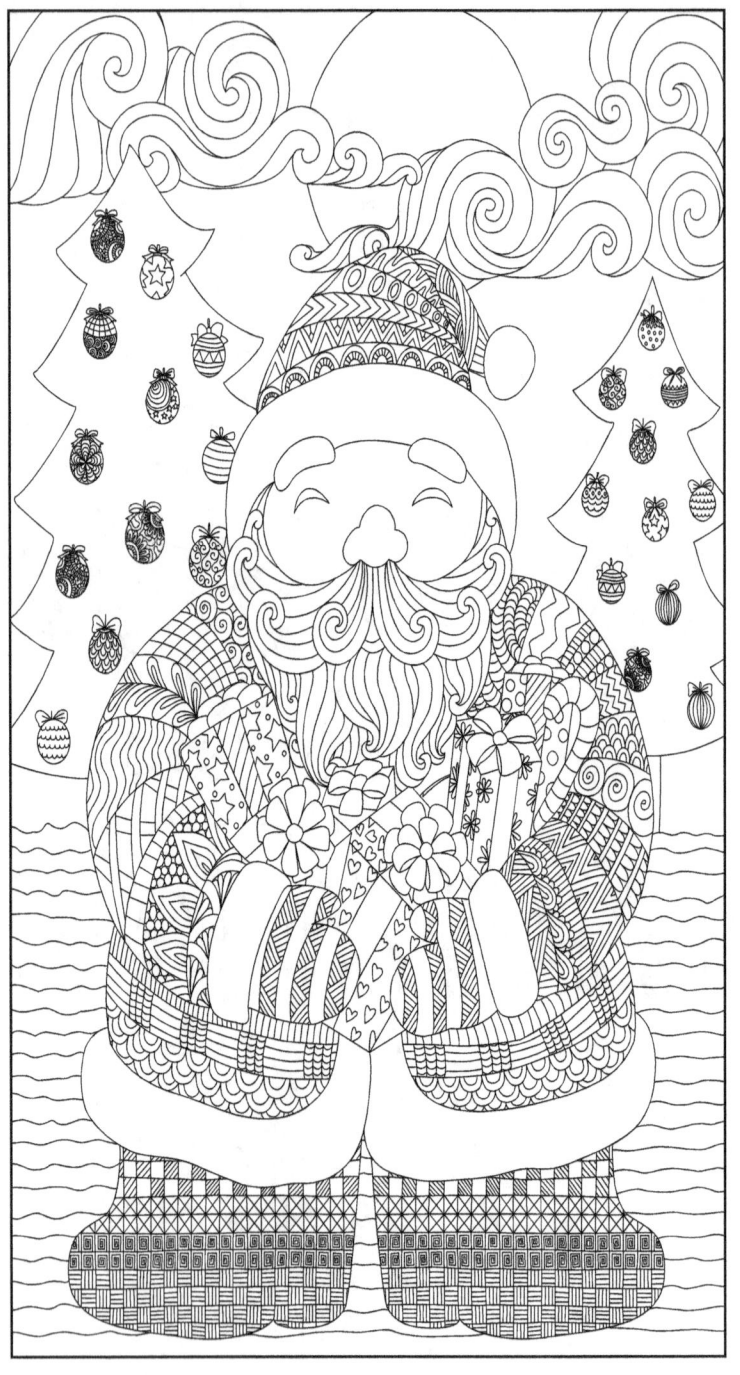

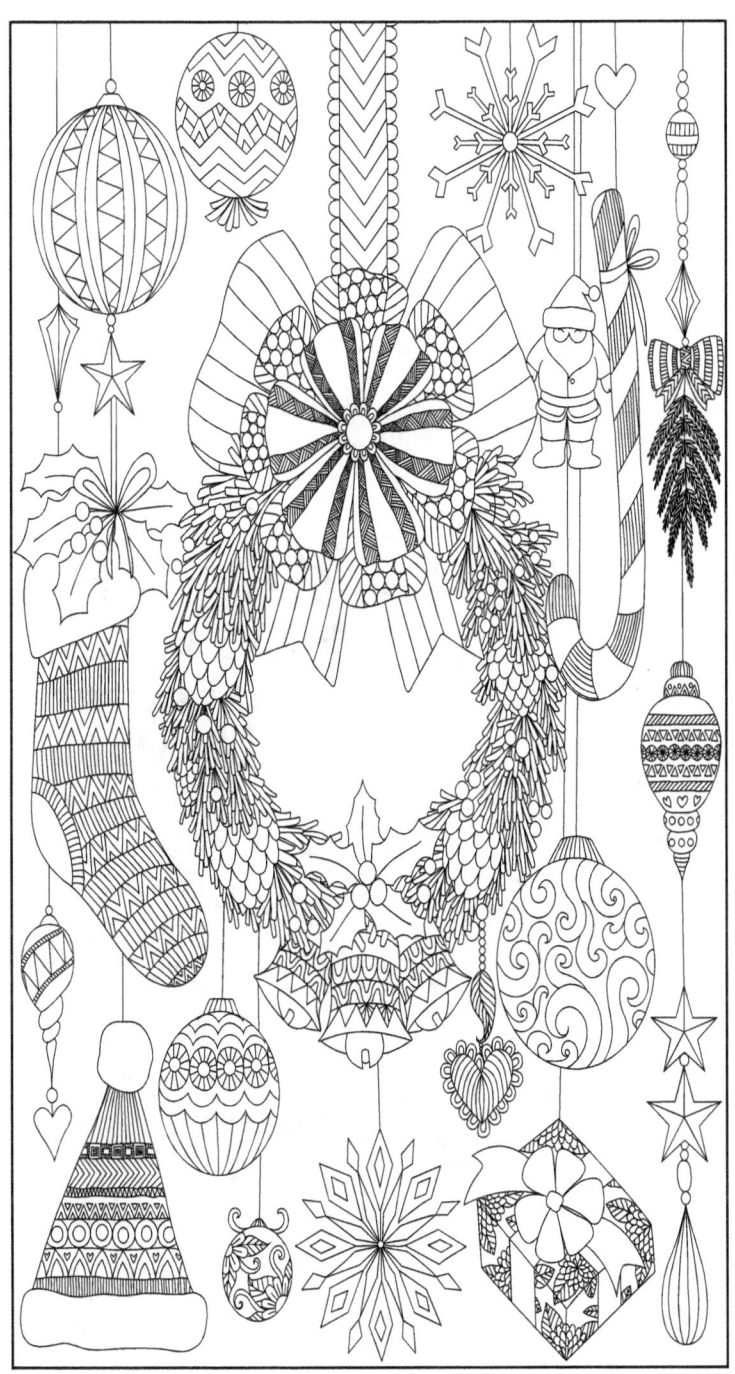

Deck the Halls

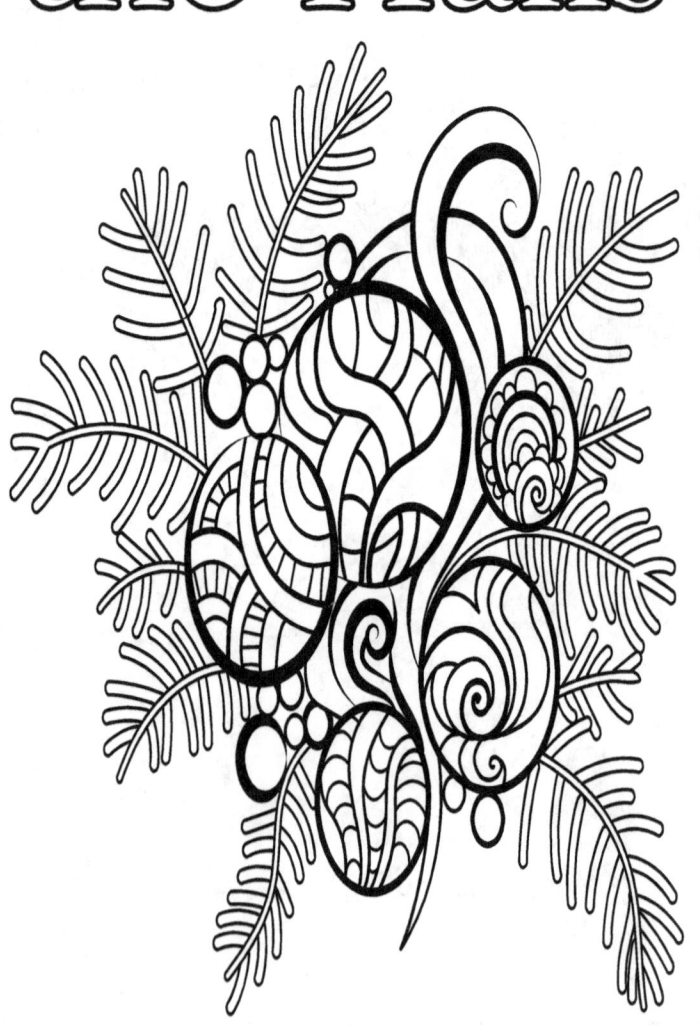

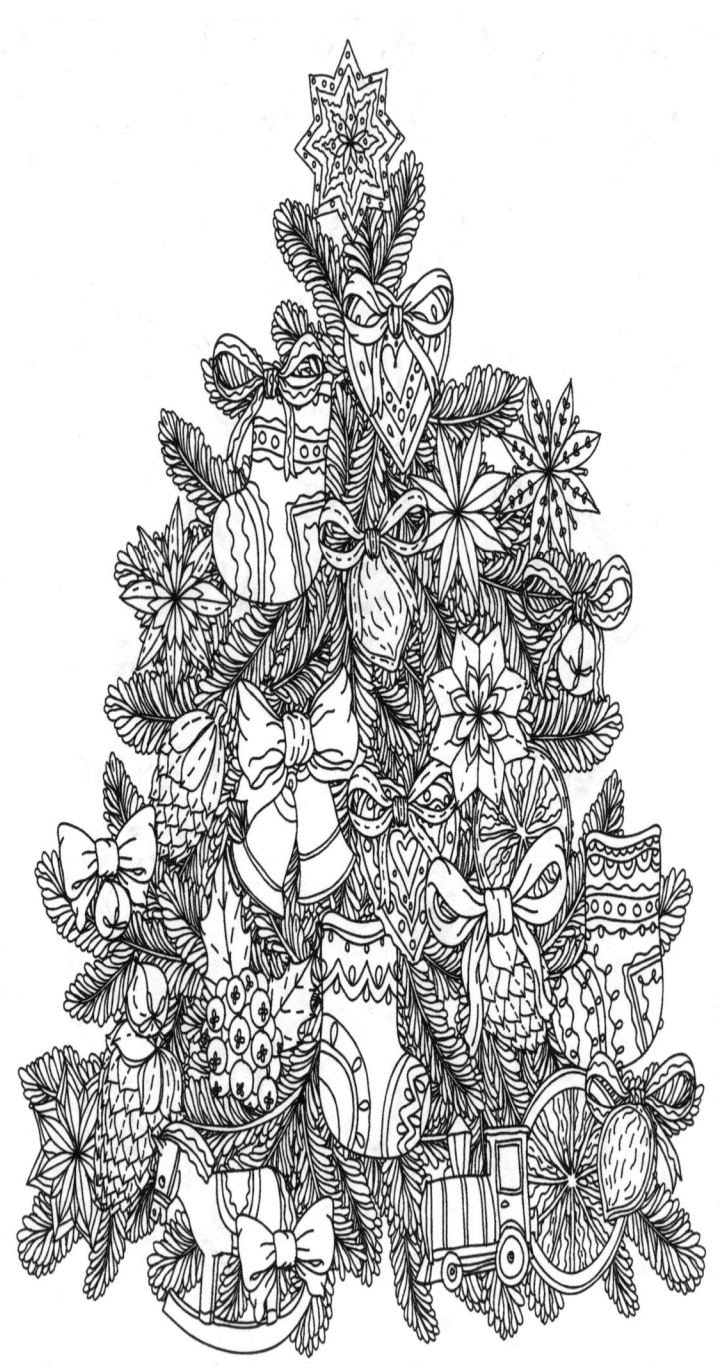

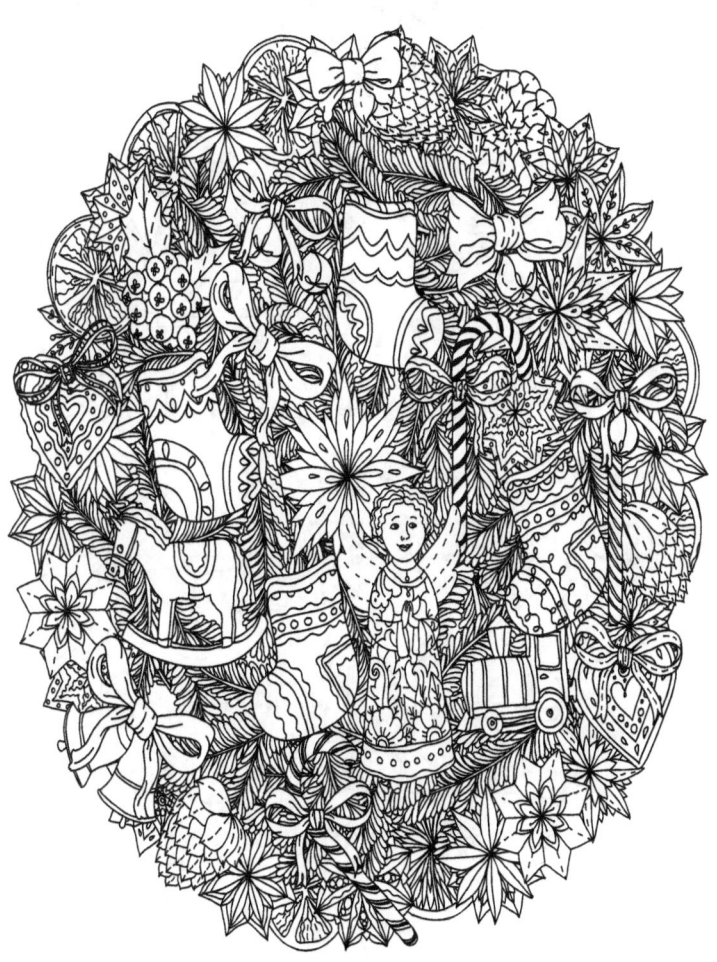

BELIEVE

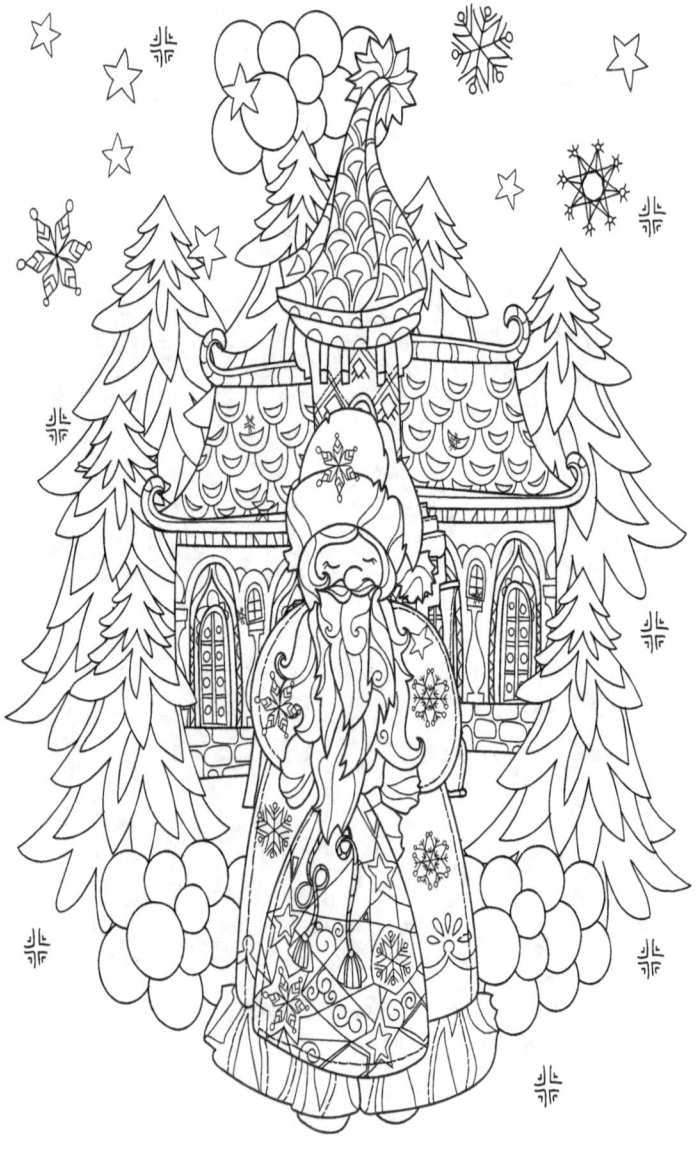

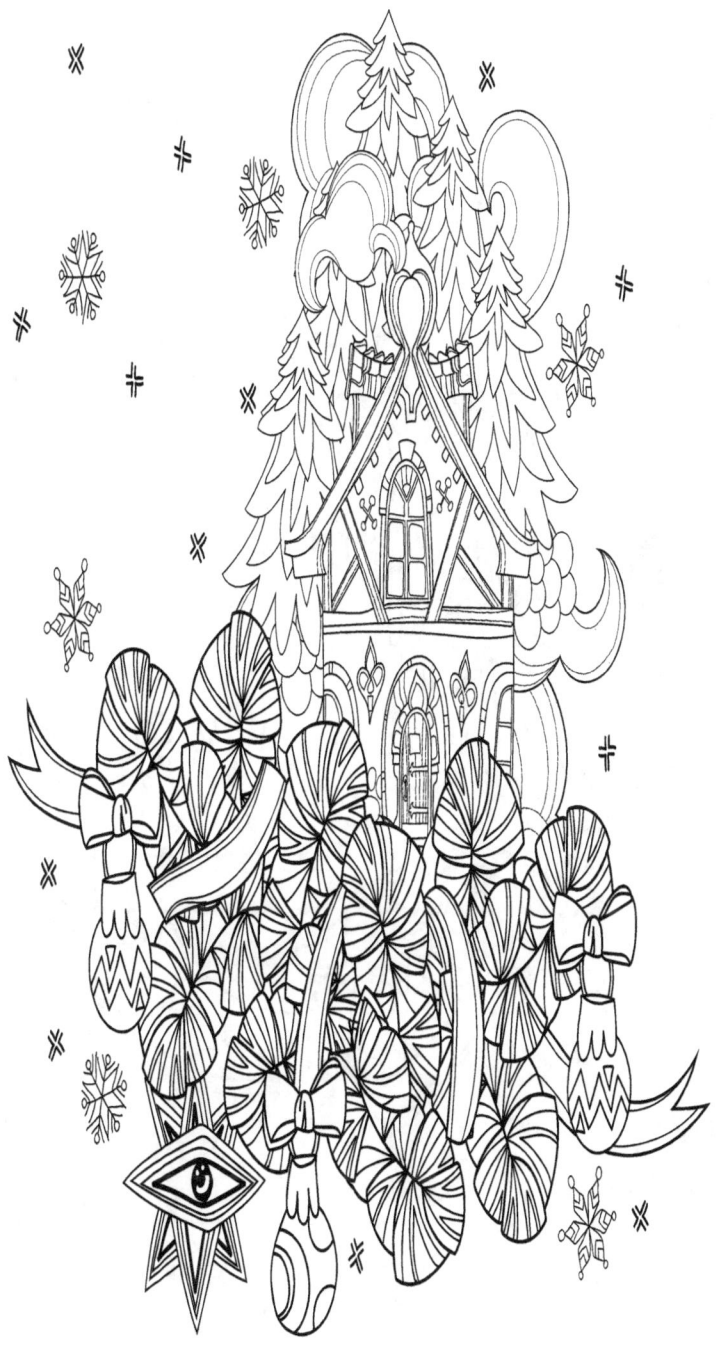

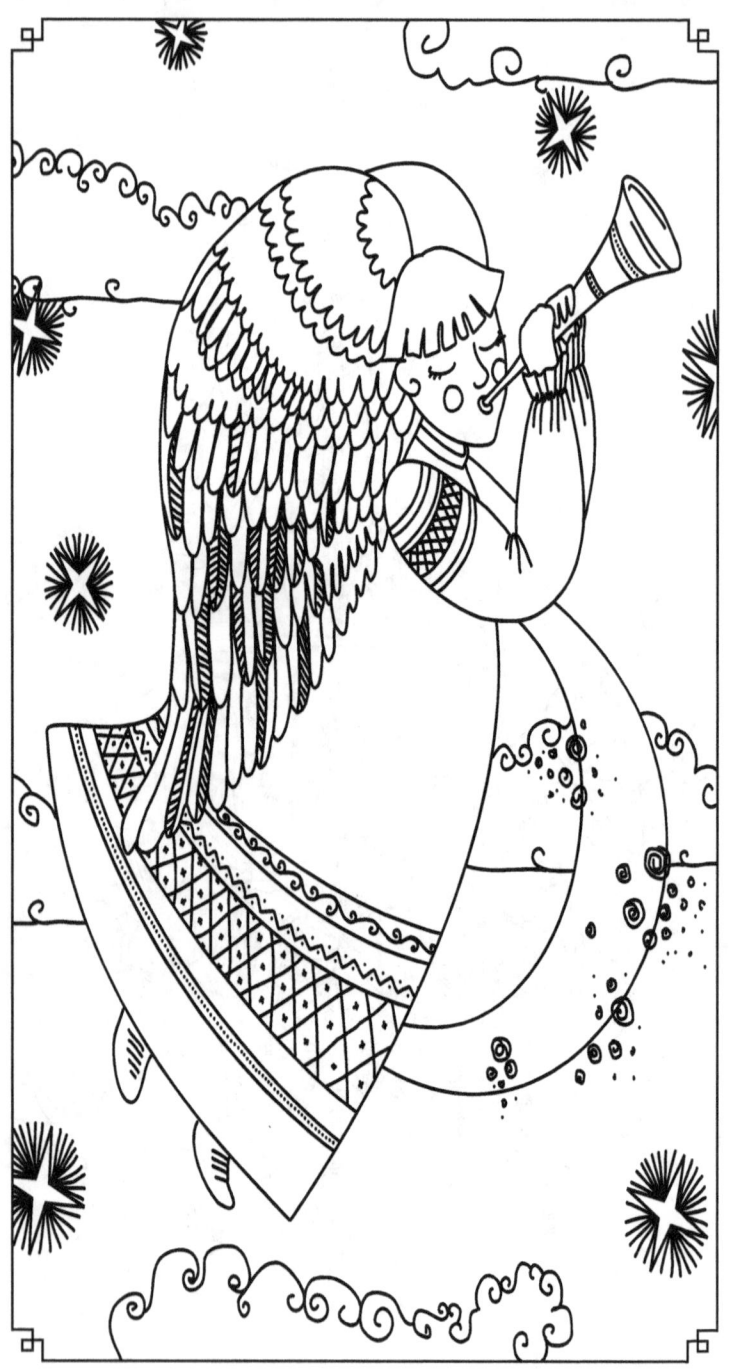

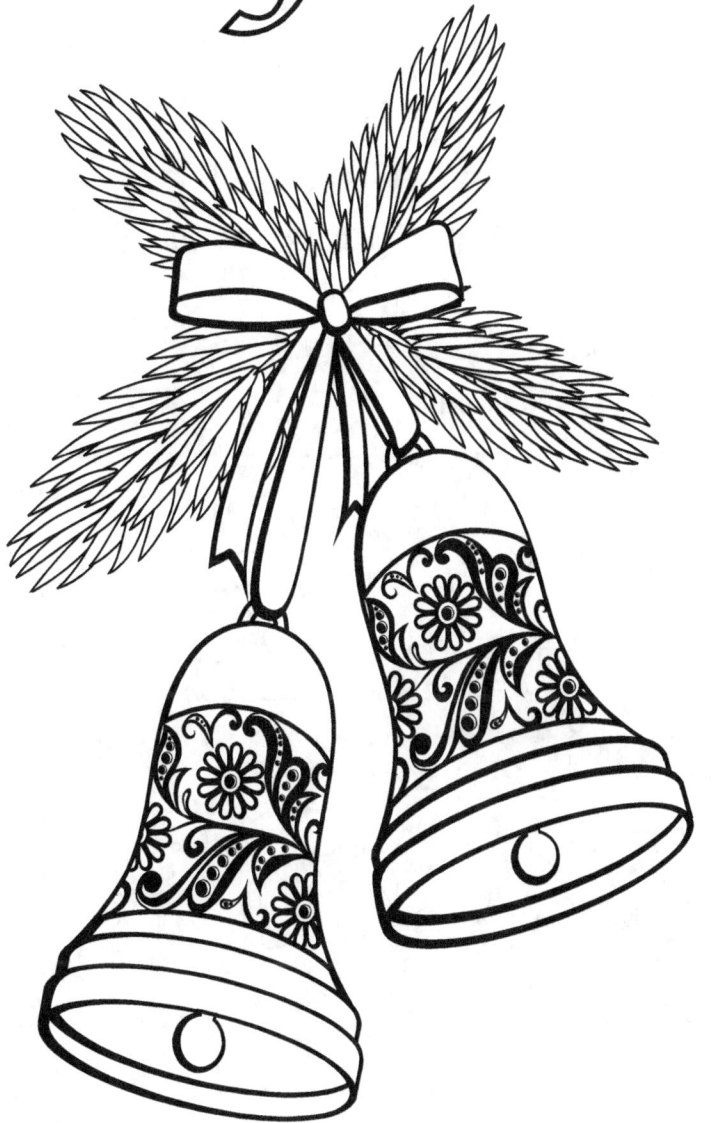

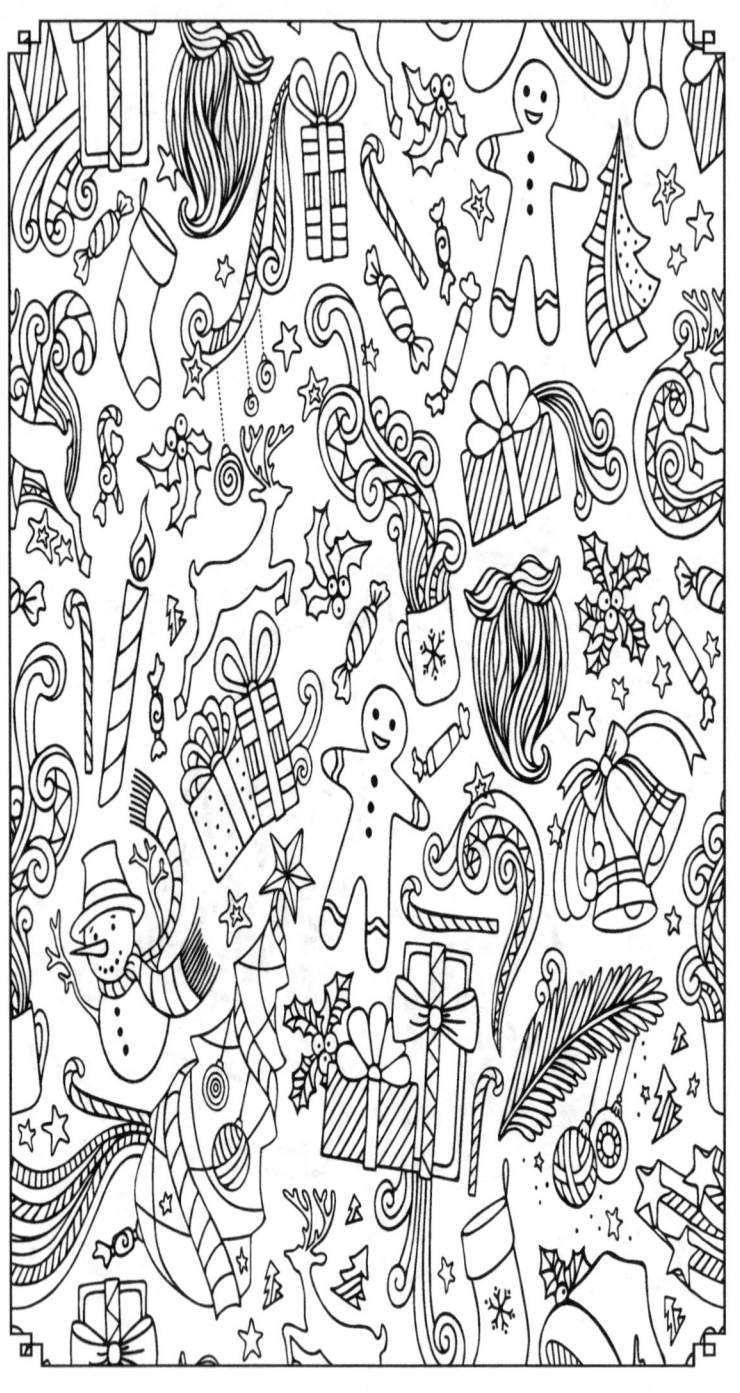

May this Christmas be bright and cheerful!

Ho! Ho! Ho!

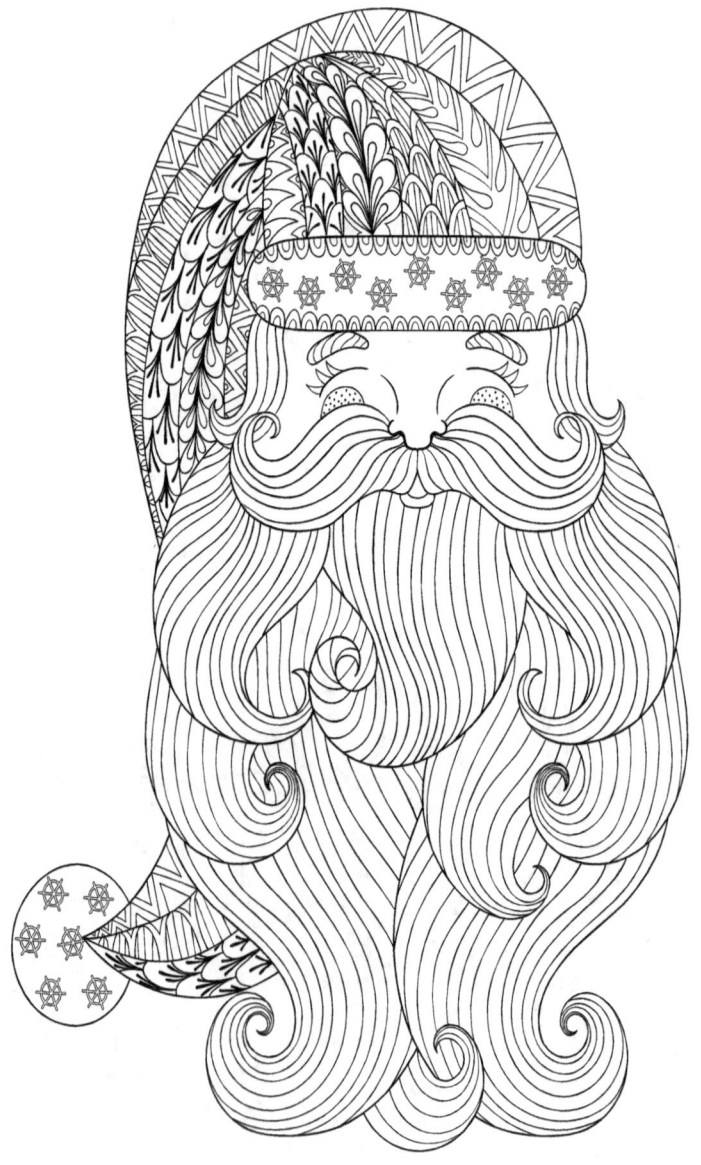

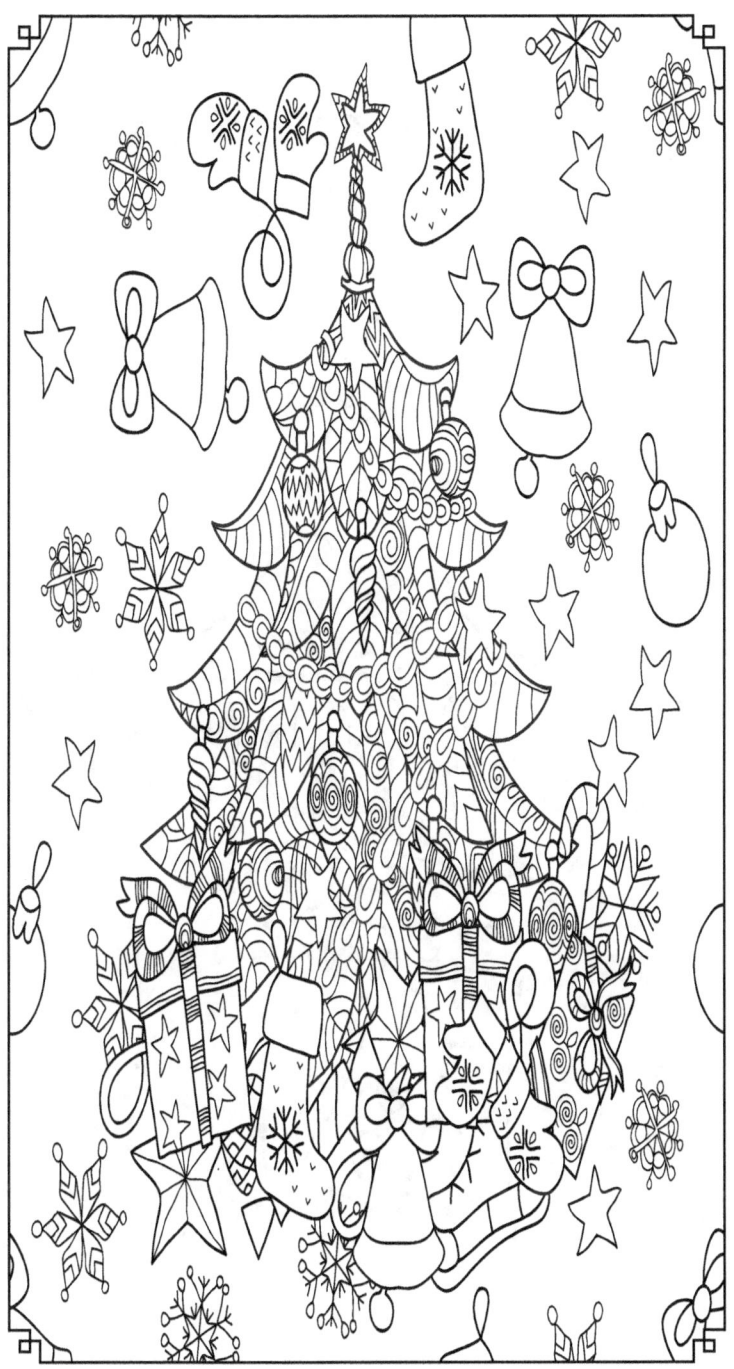

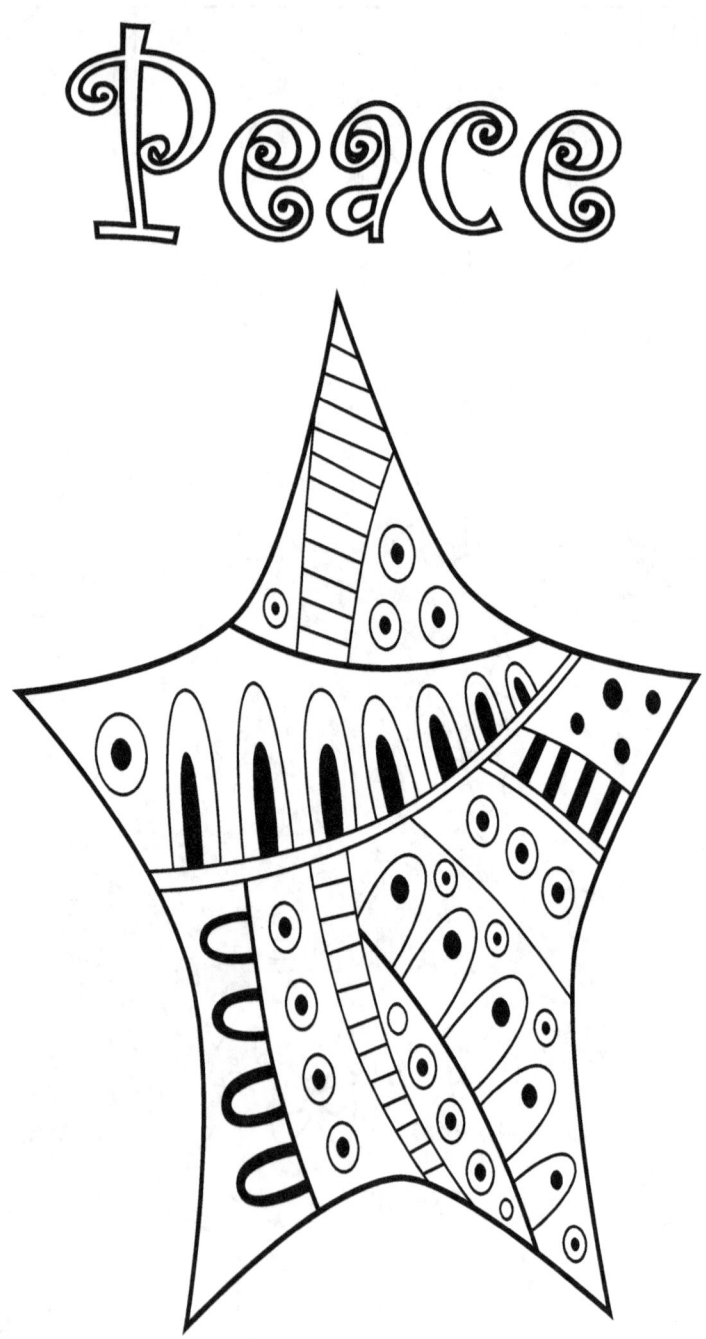

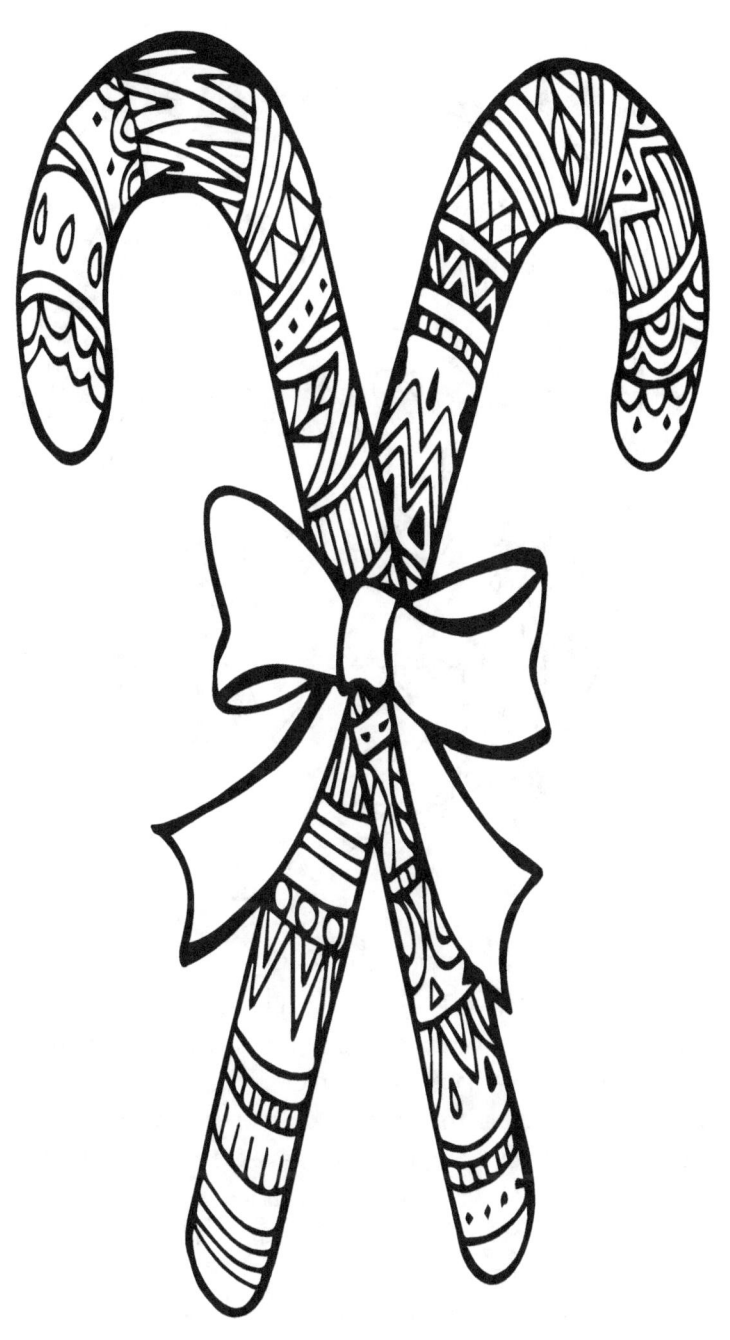

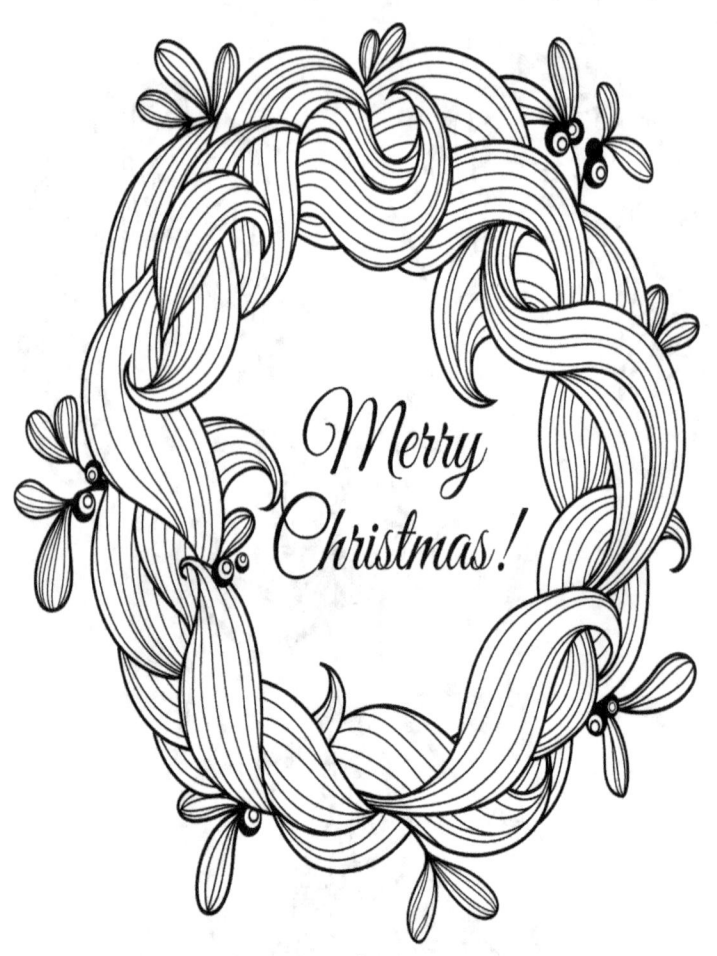

Merry Christmas!